Table of contents

preface

Introduction

Chakras

Root Chakra

Sacral Chakra

Navel Chakra

Heart Chakra

Throat Chakra

Third eye Chakra

Crown Chakra

The tools

Pranic breath

Frequency

Awareness

The inner ear

Tonal Chakra Development

The energy body

Activating the seven chakras

Slow and steady

Exercise 1. Sounding your inner tone

Exercise 2. Opening the heart

Exercise 3. Planting roots

Exercise 4. Rising sun

Exercise 5. Raising the tower

Inner tonal navigation

Exercise 6. Fire Engine

Exercise 7. Panning

Exercise 8. Front to back

Exercise 9. Full circle

Exercise 10. Figure eight

Exercise 11. Choir of angels

Full tonal control

Chakras outside of the body

Exercise 12. Earthbound

Exercise 13. The light above

Exercise 14. Whale song

Exercise 15. Pyramid of light

Exploring the energy body

Clearing "stuck" energy

Self healing

Egregores

Training aids

Voice

Musical instruments

Notes in the key of chakra

The solfeggio scale

Frequency generator

Tibetan singing bowls

Imagination

Practice helps the world go 'round

DAN SCHOEFFLER

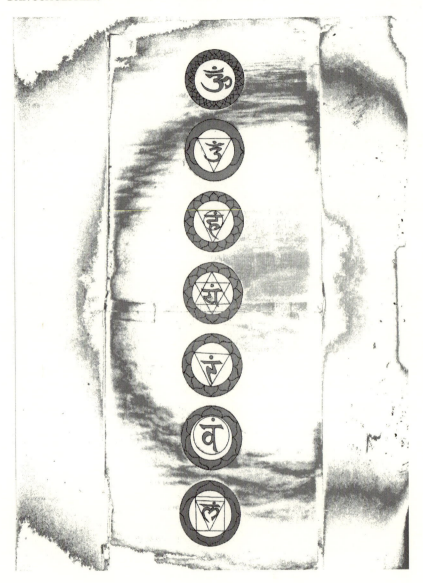

A beginner's guide to
Tonal Chakra Development
The Secret of your Inner Tone

By: Dan Schoeffler

Editor: Lucinda M. Wells
Cover art: GiYawn Lee

Acknowledgements:

I give thanks to source/creator for inspired insight and to my family and friends of which I share this reality and co-create this life with.

Relinquishment:

The publisher and the author are providing this book and its contents on an "as is" basis and make no representations or warranties of any kind with respect to this book or its contents. The publisher and the author disclaim all such representations and warranties, including but not limited to warranties of healthcare for a particular purpose. In addition, the publisher and the author assume no responsibility for errors, inaccuracies, omissions, or any other inconsistencies herein.The content of this book is for informational purposes only. Please consult with your own physician or healthcare specialist regarding the suggestions and recommendations made in this book. The use of this book implies your acceptance of this disclaimer.

Table of contents

preface

Introduction

Chakras

Root Chakra

Sacral Chakra

Navel Chakra

Heart Chakra

Throat Chakra

Third eye Chakra

Crown Chakra

The tools

Pranic breath

Frequency

Awareness

The inner ear

Tonal Chakra Development

The energy body

Activating the seven chakras

Exercise 1. Sounding your inner tone

Exercise 2. Opening the heart

Exercise 3. Planting roots

Exercise 4. Rising sun

Exercise 5. Raising the tower

Inner tonal navigation

Exercise 6. Fire Engine

Exercise 7. Panning

Exercise 8. Front to back

Exercise 9. Full circle

Exercise 10. Figure eight

Exercise 11. Choir of angels

Full tonal control

Chakras outside of the body

Exercise 12. Earthbound

Exercise 13. The light above

Exploring the energy body

Clearing "stuck" energy

Self healing

Egregores

Training aids

Voice

Musical instruments

Notes in the key of chakra

The solfeggio scale

Frequency generator

Tibetan singing bowls

Imagination

Practice helps the world go 'round

PREFACE

"If you want to find the secrets of the universe, think in terms of energy, frequency and vibration." - Nicola Tesla

I was sitting in the woods one sunny day meditating and I started thinking about the ohm, the tone that monks chant while meditating to achieve higher states of consciousness.

I suddenly realized that while I was thinking about the tone in preparation to vocalize it, the tone I was generating in my mind, with my "inner ear", was already starting to activate my heart chakra. That's when it all hit me; I already know the chakras in the body have specific frequencies, that sound is characterized by the frequency of a tone, and that I had just generated a tone in my mind that harmonized with the frequency of my heart chakra.

With this revelation I immediately brought my attention back to this "inner tone" and decided to raise the pitch. I felt a movement of energy along the path of the tone until the energy "locked into" my throat chakra. In one quick moment, as I exhaled, the energy in my heart shot up into my throat chakra as if the tone were a beacon guiding the energy to it. This astonished me and I immediately began opening up the rest of my energy body, from the root chakra to the crown chakra, and it took about 30 seconds.

I already practice meditation, but this gift, this tool that can be used sitting in meditation or standing in line, is instant gratification. Anyone can learn to open their energy body within minutes! All it takes for you to get there is "finding" your inner tone, learning to control the pitch of your inner tone, and bringing awareness to its location in your body.

I am sharing this, and the training that follows, with those who choose to hear it. I truly believe that the exercises presented in this manual will help you to fully unlock your enlightened potential.

It is also my wish to enlighten everyone who reads these words to the truth that one does not require years of meditation training and/or any type of discipleship or religion to attain higher levels of consciousness. These higher realms of awareness are given to us all when we tune into our own energetic potential with tonal awareness. Please enjoy these exercises and your new, magical, life experiences to follow.

INTRODUCTION

The human body is dependent on many things to sustain health and vitality in its function. We need water, food for nutrients, and air to breathe to sustain life. We also need exercise to ensure the proper appropriation of these elements. There is another universal element that is the foundation of all these things, it is the substance of all life, it is energy itself, it is that which all forms come from. This energy is called the quantum field by physicists, prana by vedic yogi's and chi in East Asia. This energy forms all things, is part of all things, and binds all things together.

Physicists have long known that what characterizes objects within the quantum field is vibration, and that every aspect of creation has a specific vibration. Light has a vibration, sound has a vibration, energy is vibration. Every aspect of organic and inorganic matter has a vibration and the specific rate at which anything vibrates is known as its frequency.

Musicians and physicists alike know that when you apply a specific frequency to an object that resonates at that same frequency, the object harmonizes with that frequency and becomes activated. When a musician takes a tuning fork and puts it to a stringed instrument, not only does the frequency of the tuning fork create a resonant sound from the body of the instrument, the specific string given to that frequency, or tone, also resonates. Our bodies also have specific vibrations, that is to say they also resonate at specific frequencies. Not only that but there are different frequencies for each and every organ in our body. The central nervous system, every organ, every cell in your body, abides in the quantum field as a vibration and is connected to the quantum field through the energy centers in the body known as chakras.

Light and sound are both manifestations of frequencies within the quantum field that are variable, they can both be expressed at different frequencies. Light represents its frequencies in colors, red has a different frequency than blue. The frequencies of sound are represented as tone, an (A note) has a different frequency than a (D note), just as the root chakra has a different frequency than the heart chakra. Vibration, light, and sound are all frequencies manifested through the quantum field and as such can be tuned to resonate with anything else in the quantum field including any organ in your body.

The techniques that follow are given to train your inner ear and your awareness to resonate with the specific frequencies in your body thereby being able to heal, refresh, and revitalize any aspect of your body you choose. The health benefits of bathing your body with the pranic energy of the quantum field are immeasurable. As pranic energy begins to flow more freely through the body it allows the chakra system to open even further and expand the reach of your energy body. When all of the chakras are open, one experiences complete bliss and begins to see the true nature of reality.

This is my wish for you, I sincerely believe that we are much more powerful than we were led to know, and the more of us in the know, the better off we all are. In the pages that follow we will look more into the attributes of each chakra and the emotions and bodily systems related to them. We will also talk more about the nature of frequency and some of its applications.

The tonal chakra development system presented here contains several techniques using visualization, breath-work, and meditation, that will allow you to tune your inner ear to the frequencies of your energy body, bringing harmony into your life...enjoy.

CHAKRAS

Chakras are energy centers connecting the nervous system to the energy body (the magnetic field) of a human being. Each chakra has a color, a frequency, an emotional characteristic, and correlating organs in the body. There are nine primary chakras we will be discussing, seven major chakras in the body and two outside the body. The earth star chakra is located under the feet and is for grounding and connecting to the planet and the soul star chakra shines like your own personal sun. The soul star is found above the crown chakra and connects us to the higher realms of consciousness, spirit, and the cosmos. Communication with angels and spirit guides becomes possible with activation of the higher chakras. This is where you can access the akashic records, astral travel, and even bilocate.

There are even more chakras that extend into higher dimensions but for the practices that follow we will be focusing primarily on the seven major chakras within the body along with the earth star chakra and soul star chakra respectively. Our physical body is only part of a bigger picture, it is the representation of the energy body in the quantum field.

The chakras connect our nervous system to our energy bodies which in turn connect us to the quantum field. Chakras are amazing little balls of energy that interface with the body through the nervous system which then sends this energy to the organs. These energy centers are essentially filters for cognitive input perceived in our reality, everything external that is input into our consciousness is perceived energetically. When the chakras are open and energy is flowing freely in the body the organs are bathed in light and function optimally and the body feels open and energetic. When the chakras are blocked, inhibiting the flow of energy in the body, there is felt discomfort, fatigue, and emotional discontent.

Our minds play a big part In the picture as well because it is as we perceive that we allow different vibrations of energy in. When we perceive the vibrations of beauty and light and translate it into joy and happiness, then the emotional content is vibrating high enough that it passes through the chakras easily. What we perceive as a lower vibration such as fear or guilt will get stuck in the energy body until it is consciously removed or it will take hold as an ailment or a mental or emotional blockage of some sort.

The emotional content of our perceptions have a specific frequency as well, and a correlating chakra. We find the quality of love in the heart chakra for example. When the chakras are clear all of the organs in the body function optimally and there is mental clarity and emotional well being. When all of the chakras are completely clear and fully open at the same time bliss and enlightenment are experienced.

Meditation and breath-work are essential tools for releasing blockages in the chakras. We meditate to deeply relax the body and go inward, paying attention to the energy we feel and the breath. We breathe energy into the area of our body where there is a blockage and harmonize with the vibration of that local area or organ. As you begin to become more aware of this process you will notice that as you breathe up the spinal cord the vibration of your inner ear also rises in pitch. This is because the breath tunes us into the energy body, which is a field of vibration as well. So we set our inner tone to the frequency of a given chakra and breathe pranic energy into the chakra, energizing and opening the chakra.

What we are going to learn to do here is use our inner ear as a sort of pitch control to set a tone to harmonize with the vibration of a given chakra and then allow the breath to guide energy directly to the associated chakra. As the chakra opens we learn to release old energy on our exhale, and fill up with new energy on our inhale, feeling expansion of your energy with every breath. We will learn to ground our energy body to the Earth as we open up to the energy of the cosmos, bringing heaven and earth together.

This is the true aim of these practices, when you become an open channel for universal energy, mystical experiences become inevitable. Worry not, the pressures of daily life are like a cocoon that you are breaking free from with every expansion of energy to emerge as the butterfly you were meant to be.

Let's begin by covering the seven major chakras and their properties. We'll start with the root chakra and move up vibrationally to the crown chakra. We will discuss their emotional and physical attributes as well as their colors and frequencies. From there we begin to practice training the inner ear to harmonize with these frequencies. While your intuition and awareness will guide you to the proper frequency for healing and growth, the frequencies of the chakras, and their correlating tones of the solfeggio scale, are presented in the descriptions that follow. The solfeggio scale is an ancient six note scale, closely related to the chakras, believed to have healing properties and invoke mystical experiences. Use your intuition and have fun.

"Each of the seven chakras are governed by spiritual laws, principles of consciousness that we can use to cultivate greater harmony, happiness, and well-being in our lives and in the world". - Deepak Chopra

Muladhara

ROOT CHAKRA

Color: Red.

Chakra frequency: 432 Hz.

Solfeggio frequency: 396 Hz.

Location: Base of the spine.

Characteristics: Physical identity, stability, grounding.

The root chakra is the first of the seven major chakras in the body. It is the foundation of the expansion of light into the upper chakras leading us to enlightenment and the experience of higher dimensions. This chakra is found at the base of the spine and is responsible for the energy to the lower back, lower spine, kidneys, and bladder. If the body is experiencing difficulties in any one of these areas then opening and clearing the lower chakra will initiate the healing of that area.

Our basic needs for food, water and shelter are also held within the root chakra. This chakra is concerned for our safety even though it's where we find the ability to be fearless. Confidence and expression of the divine feminine nature of our being begin to blossom as we grow our roots. We connect our physical body to the planet through opening this chakra and grounding our energy. Keeping the root chakra clear of any energetic stagnation helps to keep us from experiencing blockages in any of the other chakras above it.

Svadhishthana

SACRAL CHAKRA

Color: Orange.

Location: Just below the belly button.

Chakra Frequency: 480 Hz.

Solfeggio Frequency: 417 Hz.

Characteristics: Sensuality, pleasure, well-being.

The sacral chakra is the pleasure center of the body. It's also known as "the seat of emotions" because it uses our mental and emotional experience to navigate our perceptions of reality. The sacral chakra is found about 2" below the belly button. It is the chakra responsible for genital function and the lymphatic system. In the body the sacral chakra is the center responsible for sensation, an open sacral chakra will promote a healthy functioning of the sex organs and a general feeling of pleasure in the body.

It will allow the lymphatic system to flow freely, easily removing toxins from our body. Mentally and emotionally, the sacral chakra is where we find our dreams and fantasies, this is where we build our wishes to be turned into reality and then manifested through the naval chakra. Our sense of confidence and well-being are also ruled by the sacral chakra. When it is open we become less self-conscious and more open in our relationships. We live life authentically and experience the world around us in a brighter light.

DAN SCHOEFFLER

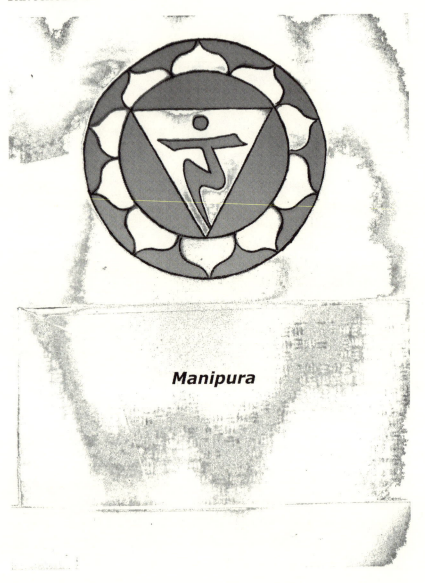

Manipura

NAVEL CHAKRA

Color: Yellow.

Location: The abdomen, extending the navel to the sternum.

Chakra Frequency: 528 Hz.

Solfeggio Frequency: 528 Hz.

Characteristics: Self-esteem, mental courage, manifestation.

The navel chakra is responsible for our personal identity and self-expression. It is also the energy powerhouse of the body. Matter turns into energy and thought to action in the sacral chakra. The manifestation of our needs and desires are the gift of this expressive energy center.

The navel chakra rules our digestive system, it is connected to the stomach, pancreas, and the liver. When this chakra is open it provides healing energy and sustains vitality to these organs. The lower back and the muscles are also under the direction of the navel chakra, a healthy flow of energy to the naval chakra promotes a strong core as a foundation for physical activity. As the chakra of the intellect, its health directly affects our level of mental courage and our ability to acquire and use knowledge. The naval chakra is also the chakra of emotional well-being, confidence and self-esteem are high with a healthy navel chakra and we become emotionally well balanced through this open energy center.

DAN SCHOEFFLER

"The most successful people are often very intuitive. Conscientiously or unconsciously, they follow their gut feelings. Following our intuition puts us in the flow - a very alive, productive, and desirable state." - Shakti Gawain

A BEGINNER'S GUIDE TO TONAL CHAKRA DEVELOPMENT

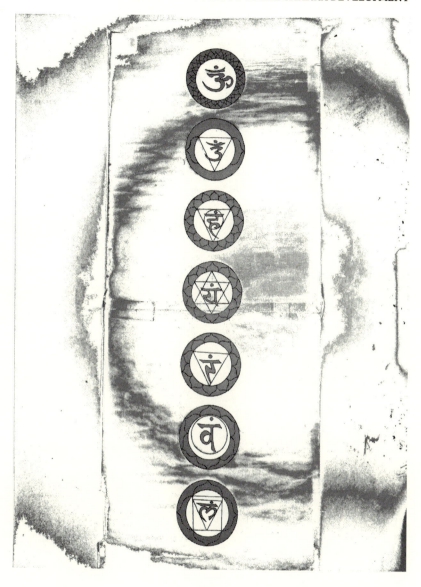

DAN SCHOEFFLER

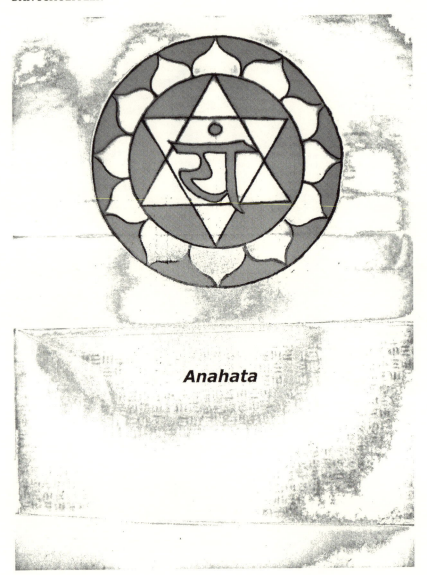

Anahata

HEART CHAKRA

Color: Green.

Location: Middle of the chest, between the breasts.

Chakra Frequency: 639 Hz.

Solfeggio Frequency: 594 Hz.

Characteristics: Unconditional love, compassion, emotional stability, connection.

The heart chakra at its core is love, it is the center of your being and it bridges the gap between your physical and spiritual energies. It is the fourth chakra in the body, connecting the lower chakras, associated with survival and navigating the stresses of everyday living, to the higher chakras, where we begin to live in love and compassion and experience bliss and enlightenment. As the lower chakras fulfill the needs of the body, they build a strong foundation on which the heart chakra can easily open, addressing the needs of the heart, and paving the way for spiritual attunement.

The physical heart, the cardiac nerve plexus and the thymus gland are wards of the heart chakra, this is why we get "butterflies' 'when we get nervously excited, especially about love. The whole area of the chest, as well as the arms and shoulders, receive energy from the heart chakra. Add to that our lungs, our heart rate cannot escape our breath rate, and in meditation we use the breath to calm the heart. A strong heart, peak blood circulation, and a healthy immune system are benefits of a clear heart chakra, plus high lung capacity and upper body flexibility for greater expression of the love that we are. The heart chakra allows us to grow lovingly into an easy connection to ourselves, others, and to nature. We feel more free and sociable, balancing reason and emotion and finding ways to work together.

Love and compassion are the primary traits of the heart chakra. While we create healthy boundaries for ourselves, we radiate loving energy from within allowing us to feel acceptance. We find expansive peace and our spirit begins to reveal itself to our conscious awareness.

Love and fear are both potentials of the heart but when we choose love, we let go, we forgive, and we transcend the ego, leading us to a life of peace and acceptance of the world around us.

"Who could refrain that had a heart to love, and in that heart to make love known".- William Shakespeare

A BEGINNER'S GUIDE TO TONAL CHAKRA DEVELOPMENT

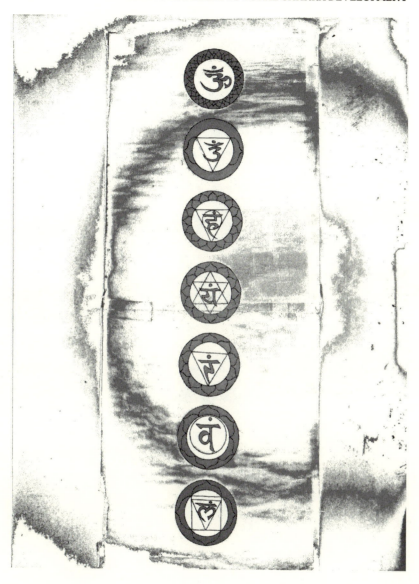

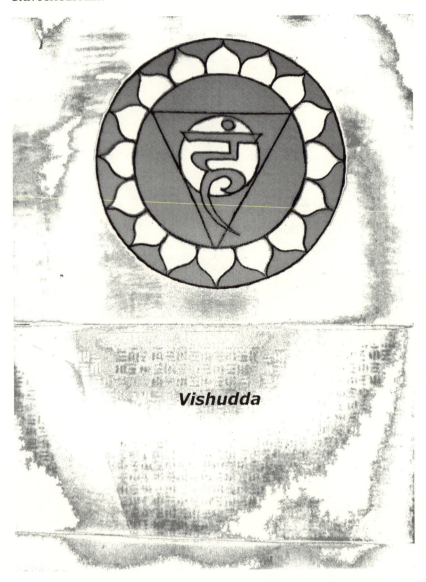

Vishudda

THROAT CHAKRA

Color: Aquamarine blue.

Location: Center of the neck in the throat area.

Chakra Frequency: 672 Hz.

Solfeggio Frequency: 741 Hz.

Characteristics: Communication, self-expression, energetic gateway to higher chakras.

The throat chakra is like a valve for energy to flow from the lower to upper chakras and vice versa, especially the flow of energy between the heart and the upper chakras of the third eye. We can freely express our authentic self with mental clarity when this chakra is open, allowing these energies to flow through. When energy gets stuck here it is felt as emotional disturbance and mental fog and can be felt as a pain in the neck. Located in the middle of the throat, this chakra can be felt coming out of the front of the throat and in from the back of the throat at a downward angle. A sensation of openness is felt from the upper respiratory to the throat when this chakra is activated.

The throat chakra is also connected to the brachial and the pharynx and rules the palate as well. The tongue, jaws, and mouth all connect to this chakra, also the neck and shoulders. This chakra supports the thyroid gland, which regulates energy by growth, metabolism, and temperature. Of all the chakras it is the one in closest communication with the body. We can use the sound of the throat to open and tune other chakras. Non verbal communication is also a facet of the throat chakra.

This is where we connect with the ethereal realm, this is where we find our intuition and also our purpose. It is the gateway to the upper chakras and connects the heart to the brain, processing information from the other chakras to be understood and applied to life in a useful and healthy manner. It is through the throat chakra that we begin to communicate with our higher selves.

"Speak with integrity. Use the power of your word in the direction of truth and love." - Don Miguel Ruiz

A BEGINNER'S GUIDE TO TONAL CHAKRA DEVELOPMENT

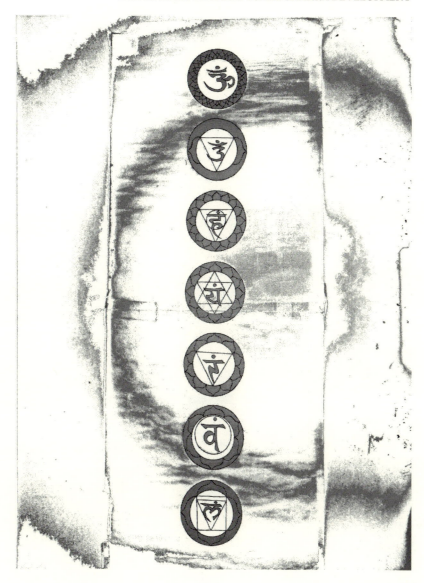

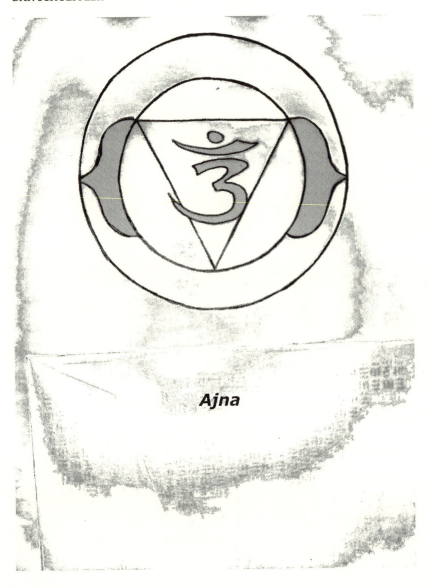
Ajna

THIRD EYE CHAKRA

Color: Indigo.

Location: Middle of the eyebrows.

Chakra Frequency: 720 Hz.

Solfeggio Frequency: 852 Hz.

Properties: Perception, awareness, psychic ability.

While the throat chakra can be called the bridge between the mind and the body, imagine the third eye as our connection between heaven and earth. This is where we experience psychic phenomena such as clairvoyance and clairaudience. We also glean inspiration, and our true purpose from our inner knowledge through this chakra. Milestones are attained in our spiritual growth when we start working with the third eye. We find this chakra parallel to the eyebrows in the center of the forehead. It encompasses the pineal gland, which can be felt tingling in the center of the head along with the brow, when this chakra is activated.

The pineal gland is responsible for our bio-rhythms and is more active at night as it determines our awake and sleep times. People's eyes are said to sparkle when the pineal gland is activated and energy is running freely through this chakra. The pituitary gland and carotid nerve plexus are also supported by the third eye as well as the brain, forehead, brow, eyes, and nose. We may experience headaches, facial pressure, blurry vision, and mental fog when there is blockage in the third eye. It is the chakra of thinking and understanding of symbolisms, with an open third eye chakra we receive information effortlessly through our higher will and discover more mental endurance and better memory. Vivid dreams are common and our imagination and visualization capacity is greatly enhanced.

The smooth functioning of this chakra will bring us emotional depth and inner peace. We find tranquility in our awareness of a divine plan unfolding in our lives. New levels of intuition and clarity bring our spirit to transcend duality, to see past polarity and adopt a witness consciousness when viewing life around us. The third eye creates harmony between the left and right brain hemispheres, marrying creative thinking and logic for an enhanced vision of our lives. Living aligned with our true nature and understanding the deeper meanings of situations and life in general as intuition grows into psychic ability.

"The light of the body is the eye: if therefore thine eye be single, thy whole body shall be full of light."
- Jesus (Matthew 6:22)

A BEGINNER'S GUIDE TO TONAL CHAKRA DEVELOPMENT

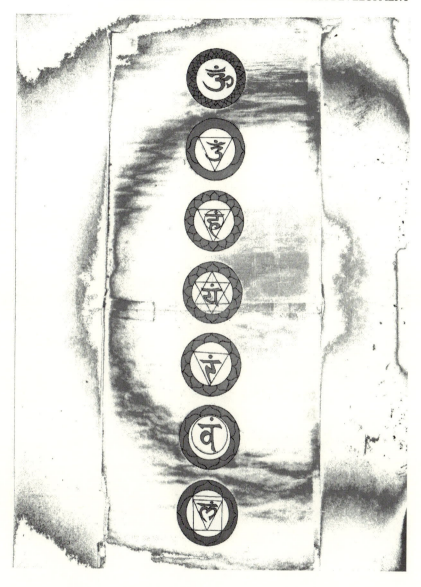

Sahasrara

CROWN CHAKRA

Color: Violet.

Location: Top of the head.

Chakra Frequency: 768 Hz.

Solfeggio Frequency: 963 Hz.

Properties: Enlightenment, universal awareness, bliss.

The Crown chakra rests at the top of the chakra tower in the body. It allows energy to flow from the higher chakras to the other chakras below it and ground down to Earth creating a bridge of energy through the body. This chakra connects us to the divine where we find unity and connectedness to everything in the universe. Peace, joy and bliss are the language of the crown chakra. The intellect is absent but there is a sense of knowing, an understanding of a grander scheme and greater meaning in life. The ego must be transcended, and we must accept intrinsically the unity of the universe and everything in it, to abide in the energy of the crown chakra.

Our release into this "knowing" is where we find the "zero point" field, where we truly become that which is all that is. We go beyond contemplation to realization of the zero point field when we open the crown chakra and we feel as if we're floating in the space of all that is. We give to and receive energy from the field through the crown. When our connection to this energy is unobstructed we radiate perfect peace and live in vibrant health. Our bodies enjoy a calm and sensitive nervous system with alert reflexes and peak physical health. We can find a sense of completion, we learn to let go and surrender to our higher purpose and an acceptance of everything as it is.

People with open and active crown chakras are sensitive, aware or "awake", and are spiritually powerful and emotionally balanced. Our awareness expands and our divine birthright of intuitive and joyful knowing begins to lead us from the energies of our instincts for survival to a life led from the heart, a life of selflessness, service, and spiritual growth. As we taste our divinity, mystical and spiritual experiences become commonplace and we begin to know the highest levels of reality. It is through deep meditation, contemplation, and prayer, that we strengthen our ability to experience these realms.

"The key to growth is the introduction of higher dimensions of consciousness into our awareness." - Lao Tzu

THE TOOLS

There are three key elements to the Tonal Chakra Development system, the breath, the inner ear, and awareness. With abdominal breathing we guide pranic energy to the location of our body, established by the awareness of the frequency of our inner tone and harmonizing with the frequency of the chakra. When our inner tone harmonizes with the frequency of a given chakra we become aware of a sensation in our body at the location of the chakra.

Harmonizing our inner tone with that of a given chakra will generate a sensation of activation but it is when we pull the energy into the chakra with abdominal breathing that we begin to clear and open up the chakra. This harmony allows energy to expand and heal any correlating physical, mental, and emotional blockages associated with the chakra. A minimal understanding of these three elements, breath, tone, and awareness, will help you build a strong foundation for your energy work.

PRANIC BREATH

Prana, in Sanskrit, is life force. That which sustains us on a cellular and nuclear level. The breath of life, pranic breathing allows us to saturate our being with this life force, creating health and harmony in the body, mind, and spirit. When we draw breath into the body normally, we are focused on our heartbeat and upper chest, drawing most of the air into the top of our lungs on the inhale while our lower lungs remain much less active. If we wish to directly engage with the life force that surrounds us (the pranic energy that sustains all life) we must learn to activate the lower portion of our lungs through abdominal breathing.

Abdominal breathing is achieved by focusing on the seat of your chalice, the bottom of the tailbone, and then drawing the breath from the base of the spine, at the tailbone, up through the lower abdomen and into the bottom of the lungs while inhaling through the nose. Pranic breathing is applying a cyclical rhythm to the timing of the breath. A specific duration of time, or count, is given to the inhale, the exhale, and a hold when the lungs are full and again when they are completely empty. First we direct pranic energy to a specific point in our body with our breath then we suspend the breath in that location momentarily, revitalizing and clearing out any stuck energy in that area of the body. We then exhale for a given count to expel any stuck energy from our field.

An example of a pranic breath cycle could be to inhale for a six count, bringing energy into the body and suspending the breath for a three count, saturating a given area of the body with that energy. Then we slowly exhale and release any stuck energy for another six counts as we allow it to flow freely through that area of the body and make sure to expel the air completely from the lungs. We then suspend the breath for another three counts to begin the cycle again.

We will use both abdominal and pranic breathing techniques for the tonal chakra development system to gain full awareness of our energy body. As we begin to feel the pranic energy awaken in the body we can then direct our attention to root chakra, located at the base of the spine. We inhale into the tailbone allowing our lower abdomen to expand and open the root chakra on the exhale. Then we continue to pull the energy up the spine while inhaling through the nose as we direct our attention to the second chakra, the sacral chakra, and repeat the cycle. As this energy then travels up the body It opens up each of the chakras along the spinal column and up through the top of the head.

The aim of pranic breathing is to activate each chakra in turn as we fill our bodies with pranic energy from the base of our spine to the top of our head. As each chakra is open, we feel the energy in that area expand and our body becomes wonderfully relaxed and open to the quantum field. As we breathe into these chakras and open them, the associated organs and areas of the body that receive this cleansing and nurturing pranic energy are replenished to optimal function.

When we master this breathing of energy through the body and do it on a regular basis, we are opening and releasing any physical, emotional, and mental trauma. Through this cleansing process we feel lighter, happier, and have greater vision and clarity. The goal of meditation and pranic breathing together is opening and maintaining balance in the chakras, living and enjoying a more full and authentic life, experiencing your highest abilities, deepest connections, and most desirable timelines. The goal of the Tonal Chakra Development system is to give you a tool to guide this energy wherever you want to in the body, whenever you want to, and wherever you are, using your inner tone as a guide.

"Breathing is the greatest pleasure in life." - Giovanni Papini.

FREQUENCY

Everything in the known physical universe has a vibration. Frequency is the rate at which a vibration occurs that constitutes a wave, either in a material, as in sound waves, or in an electromagnetic field (as in radio waves and light). We measure frequency in hertz (Hz), which is the distance between the peak of one wave to the peak of its adjacent wave in a constant vibration. If an object operates at 60 Hz, (like a light bulb), then that object, or its function, is oscillating sixty times in the duration of one second. In the case of a light bulb, the light filament literally flashes on and off 60 times within the duration of one second. Since most people only perceive light at between 50 to 60 Hz, or frames per second, the light is perceived as continuous.

Musicians and physicists know that when two objects are tuned to the same frequency and placed in close proximity, when one object is activated the other will begin to resonate as well. When a guitarist strikes a tuning fork (440 Hz) and places it on the body of their instrument, a tone is produced from the instrument. When the A string is perfectly tuned to the tuning fork (440 Hz), it will vibrate when the tuning fork is struck and held near it, even without contact to the body of the instrument. So you see any object that is tuned or harmonized at the same frequency as any other object becomes quantumly entangled in a parasympathetic relationship, exchanging information instantly.

In radio waves this information is carried at the peak of every wave, when we assign a radio station a frequency and you tune your radio to it, you instantly receive the information from the source of the signal. The signal does not start from its point of origin and end up where it is received, rather the wave already exists at both ends at the same time. So when we open our chakras we are just tuning our ' 'receiver" to the given frequency of a quantum "radio station" instantly.

Our bodies have a specific frequency, our organs, our cells, and our thoughts and emotions, all have individual and specific frequencies as well. When we get blood transfusion, or an organ transplant, we have to make sure the frequencies of the donor are compatible to that of the recipient. Different blood types have different frequencies. When it comes to the quantum field, we are talking about the mother of all radio stations as it is the origin and foundation of all delineations of frequency that exist in the known universe.

It is the frequencies of the quantum field that we will be applying to the techniques that follow. With our knowledge that every one of our chakras has a resonant frequency with they're related organs in the body, we begin to "tune in" to the frequency of each chakra to "receive" the quantum signal and in turn activating the chakras sending this same signal to the organs in the body and the body as a whole. This is how the healing begins.

AWARENESS

When we become aware of something we are giving it our full attention at that moment. A gust of wind may bring our awareness to the weather at that moment and the feeling of the breeze bathing our skin. We pay attention to crossing the street when we become aware of a moving vehicle. In meditation and energy work we take that awareness to the more subtle levels of energy in our bodies. Sensation is our awareness of a feeling in the body. Whether it be pain or pleasure, anxiety or peace, the sensation of openness and joy we find in love, or the feeling of contraction that comes from fear.

Awareness of the energy in our bodies requires unbroken attention to any area of the body we are focusing on at that moment. If we focus on our solar plexus and pay attention to our breath moving into this area, we become aware of a subtle sensation at our point of focus. If you imagine fingernails dragging across a chalkboard then you may experience the awareness of the same sensation in the solar plexus as well. This psychosomatic sensation is produced by the pitch you generate from your inner ear.

Awareness is an integral part of the tonal chakra development system as we will use this awareness of the subtle energies in the body, in conjunction with the tone we will consciously generate with our inner ear, to locate and open our chakras. We will bring awareness to the sensation that the tone from our inner ear creates and then adjust that tone to the location of one of the chakras.

We will also bring awareness to our breathing as we guide pranic energy, with the breath, to the chakra now identified by our inner tone. We expand our awareness of our energy body as we continue this process, opening the other chakras in our energy body. When all of our chakras are open at once our awareness is expanded to the whole body and our connection to the quantum field.

THE INNER EAR

Awareness, and mastery of the inner ear, are key elements of the tonal chakra development system. Fortunately they are natural abilities we as humans are born with and they are very easy to remember how to use. The inner ear we speak of is not the fragile bone structure of our biological ear that we use for balance. It is the imaginative ear that hears our thoughts.

We use our inner ear every time we listen to our favorite song in our head. If we can think in sentences, we can think in songs. Mastery of the inner ear is obtained when we move from the listener to the composer of the music of the mind. In music, the frequency of a tone is defined as (pitch), and musical notes are representations of their relative pitch. We are going to learn to raise and lower the pitch of our inner tone through the frequencies of 396 Hz to 963 Hz. It is within this range of frequency that we activate the seven major chakras in our body. To isolate your inner tone just relax and think of a familiar sound, it could be the garbage truck "beeping" in the morning or the sound of the microwave when your food is done. This sound that you hear could be your favorite song. The point is to use a sound, or tone, that is familiar. This will make it easy to tune into our inner ear with our awareness. Now that we have a connection with the inner ear we can begin to open it's range with this same technique, just think of a familiar tone and hear it in your imagination, then raise and lower that tone with your inner ear. Think of how an opera singer might warm up their vocal cords. Since our inner ear is free from the limitations of our vocal range we can hit those same notes to bring awareness to the range and tone of our inner ear.

A good practice to bring awareness to the range of frequency that we will use to open up the seven chakras in the body is to tune your inner ear while imagining an emergency vehicle siren, hear the siren sounding from low to high and back again, bringing your awareness to the tone as it travels back and forth along the range of the siren.

This practice will help us begin to identify the location of the chakras in our body as well. When you use your inner ear to move the tone of the siren up and down your spine you will begin to feel sensations in your body moving with it. When the tone harmonizes with the frequency of one of the chakras, say the heart chakra (594 Hz), then that chakra begins to activate. It is at that point in our practice that we will draw pranic energy with our breath into that location, and fully activate it. When the heart chakra is activated with our inner tone we feel all warm and fuzzy inside. When we draw energy into this location we feel unfettered joy, bliss, and love.

Once you get the hang of this practice you can do it anywhere and at any time, activating any or all of your chakras. Standing in line is a good time to practice. You can even harmonize your inner ear to "sing" along with your favorite song on the radio. The more we practice awareness of the sounds we hear in life through our inner ear, the more proficient we become in using our inner ear to locate and open the chakras in our body. In the exercises that follow we will bring the elements of awareness, the breath, and the inner ear together at the specific location and frequency of each of the seven chakras in the body, reinvigorating our energy body and bringing us more clarity, greater joy, and vibrant health.

When we speak of the inner ear we are talking about the innate faculty of a human being to imagine sound as if they are hearing it with they're mind. The biological inner ear refers to the semicircular canals and cochlea which form the organs of balance and hearing and are embedded in the temporal bone. The inner ear we refer to is able, with some development, to generate and listen to tonal thought forms at the same time. Like an audio speaker your inner ear uses the signal from your mind to induce an electromagnetic field that is converted to a physically qualitative vibration.

Our mind is like a radio station sending a signal. Our inner ear tunes into the signal and converts the signal to a physical vibration. In our case the physicality is sensory and operates at the subtle plane of our nervous system. When we tune to different frequencies with our inner ear we are activating different aspects of energy to locate in different areas of the body. So we sing with the mind and listen with the body as if it were one action. Re-awakening this dormant ability to tap into the source of all creation may or may not happen overnight. But with an open mind, some imagination and motivation you will learn and remember your true nature and power.

TONAL CHAKRA DEVELOPMENT

Now that we have an understanding of the energy bodies and of the components of the tonal chakra development system; (tone, pranic breath, and awareness), we can begin to put it to practice. While the exercises put forth in the tonal chakra development system can be done in a sitting, standing, or prone (lying down) position, we will start in the sitting position for descriptive purposes but you should choose whatever position is most comfortable for you. Begin by taking a moment to relax and clear your mind, then set the tone of your inner ear. "Setting the tone" is how we will describe the activation of a given frequency within the inner ear for the purpose of these exercises.

You don't need to worry much about your thoughts rambling because as soon as you set the tone in your inner ear your attention is drawn to that tone. Once you have set the tone we will ask you to raise or lower that tone to coordinate with the location of one or more of the chakras. This is your awareness at work, modulating the tone of your inner ear while feeling its effect in your body and bringing the two into harmony. At this point, while your tone is harmonizing with your chakra, we will ask you to breathe into the chakra that is being activated. When we use the word "breathe" we are talking of pranic breath, drawing energy through the body with abdominal breathing and awareness. Let's begin...

THE ENERGY BODY

We are much more than just flesh and bone. We are more than our intellect, our emotional content, and our beliefs. Beyond these qualities we are energy. Energy is the commonality in every human being, the medium of all existence, and the quality of that energy is love. Love is the language that commands the energy we are personally responsible for and the inspiration that touches the love of others. Energy itself is neutral, the same quantum energy sustaining you and me is the same energy that sustains a tree.

The hidden force that directs this energy is love, and love is a quality that every human being can manifest. Each individual is the center of their own reality in a reality of innumerable individuals. We are the energy that we see outside of ourselves and we are personalized in this quantum energy field by our energy body. Think of an egg and imagine you are the yolk, sustained by the nutrients of the amniotic fluid in a cozy bubble around you, and nurtured through the warmth and attention of the mother hen. We are the yolk and our energy body is the amniotic fluid that permeates and suspends us in a field of energy. The mother hen is love, creating and nurturing into life, a love which is of its own.

As we begin to work with our energy body, opening and clearing the seven chakras in the body, we will start physically feeling this energy on a quantum level, we will also become aware of any imbalances within our energy body. When these imbalances arise it is necessary to clear the energy that may get "stuck" in your energy body once it is released from your physical body. If a blockage is released into the energy body without clearing it then that blockage will return or show up somewhere else in the body.

The exercises in the Tonal Chakra Development system are intended to open the seven major chakras in the body, and clear old energy from the energy body. I say intended because it is our intention that creates great changes and growth in our life. The benefits of an open energy body are endless, with more clarity, greater health, and higher spiritual awareness, we naturally emerge as the authentic personalization of our true self.

Think of your energy body like your galactic vehicle, first you need to familiarize yourself with the controls, then you need to learn how to operate it. Confidence builds as you take it around the block a few times and then before you know it, driving the vehicle becomes second nature and you choose your destination and go. The destinations of your energy body are higher dimensions and, with full awareness of your energy body, you can go there.

"The key to growth is the introduction of higher dimensions of consciousness into our awareness." - Laozi

ACTIVATING THE SEVEN CHAKRAS

The exercises that follow are meant to bring new energy into our chakras as we clear out old energy that may have gotten stuck and bring balance to our body. Injury, trauma, or just having a bad day can block energy from flowing freely through your energy body. We open the chakras by removing the old energy as we bring in the new energy and then grounding the energy at the end of each exercise.

Grounding connects us to the planet and aligns the electrical energy in our bodies. We will end each exercise by bringing our awareness to the connection of our root chakra to the planet. Then we let any excess energy drain out of our body and into the center of mother earth until balance is felt throughout our body. Remember these exercises are meant as an introductory guide to tonal energy work as well as an accessory to any practice you may already be doing so feel free to improvise.

Begin each exercise in a sitting position and settle into a rhythmic abdominal breathing pattern. Again, when we say "breathe into" any location in the body in the exercises that follow we are referring to drawing pranic breath from the abdomen to the location of the tone that you have set in your inner ear. Once we draw the breath to the location of our inner tone, we will suspend the breath for as long as is comfortable, and then slowly exhale as we hold our inner tone, letting the pranic energy that we've drawn with the breath expand in the location of our awareness. This expansion will feel as if you are filling up with warm energy in the chakra you are bringing your awareness to.

The locations we will be focusing on in the exercises that follow are those of the seven chakras in the body. As you set your tone and bring awareness to your breathing, imagine that you are filling up with light as you inhale, and then feel the body relax and let any tension release as you exhale. Begin slowly, breath after breath, releasing tension where you may find it like melting an ice cube into a puddle and then feeling the puddle evaporate as your energy expands. Bit-by-bit your energy body is activated as trauma and injury erode with the tonal tides of your new abilities.

When you're chakras or are all open at the same time all of the energy centers in your body merge into one. Imagine feeling like a wonderful force of light shining forth from a core of ecstatic bliss. The light has no boundaries and the bliss beckons endless expansion to no end. There are no boundaries to eternity and we are eternal beings.

SLOW AND STEADY

The techniques of tunnel shocker development are meant to guide your awareness through the exploration of your energy body. Bitch they are not regimental, you can start where you want according to your own proficiency. Everyone is different and carries different energies accumulated from our lifetimes. We have different bodies and different personalities. We think and feel differently. We have different karma. A person who has fear trauma will need to work more on the root chakra where as a person with anger issues with struggle in opening their heart. This means that in the beginning some chakras will be easier to work with than others.

While grounding your energy is probably the most important part of any energy work, you may find it difficult opening your root chakra at first. So we will begin the first exercise by bringing your awareness to your lower chakras so you get a feeling of your inner tone interacting with your energy body. You want to find the easiest point of access to begin bringing tonal awareness to and then go from there.

An example could be that your energy opens up in your naval chakra first. You would then lower your tone until you feel energy at your sacral chakra, let it open, and then move on down to your root chakra. No matter where your energy opens first, always ground it at the beginning of each practice. You will be doing all of this instantaneously once you put it all together, but for now it's best to be free from distraction. You want to complete any exercise before doing anything else and if you have to stop, do it gently and settle your energy.

EXERCISE 1. SOUNDING YOUR INNER TONE

Step 1. Pick a quiet place and begin humming while at the same time paying attention to the vibration in your body.

Step 2. Raise and lower the tone you are humming so that you feel the vibration moving from the area in your upper chest to the area in your tailbone and repeat until you have a clear sense of the tone, moving with the vibration, up-and-down your spine.

Step 3. Listen to the tone of the humming with your inner ear until you are following the vibration up-and-down your spine and then stop humming out loud and continue to pay attention to your inner tone moving with the sensation you feel in your body.

We will begin each exercise that follows by establishing our inner tone and directing it to a specific location in our body. The point of this exercise is to learn to establish your inner tone without humming audibly. You can set your inner tone using an outside source but it is just as easy to generate the tone with your mind, like listening to a song in your head.

EXERCISE 2. OPENING THE HEART

Step 1. Begin sounding your inner tone as you did in exercise 1. Raise and lower your inner tone until you can feel the tone moving up-and-down your spine.

Step 2. Once you have established this tonal path, pay attention to your inner tone as it rises up your spinal column and hold it at the center of your chest at the point where you feel a tingling, in the area of your heart, in the middle of your chest.

Step 3. Slowly draw your pranic breath to the location of your inner tone and suspend the breath for a moment, feeling your heart chakra begin to open, then slowly exhale while keeping your inner tone harmonized to the heart chakras frequency, and letting the pranic energy fully expand into your heart chakra.

Step 4. Repeat step 3. until you feel the full expansion of your heart chakra as you continue abdominally breathing, pulling pranic energy into the location of your inner tone within your heart chakra, until it opens.

Opening the heart chakra instantly lifts your mood and raises your vibration. You will feel a sensation of openness in your chest and as you fill the heart with prana this feeling of openness will expand. Move to the next exercise once you feel the heart chakra is fully open.

EXERCISE 3. PLANTING ROOTS

Step 1. Begin again sounding your inner tone and pay attention to the pitch of your inner tone as you feel the tone lowering down your spine and then hold the tone in the area of your tailbone, becoming aware of any sensation you feel in your root chakra, and fix your attention to that area as you continue to hold your inner tone to that frequency.

Step 2. Breath into the root chakra as you hold your inner tone to its frequency. Do this by "pulling" your breath down your spine and towards your sphincter as you expand your belly. Simultaneously draw pranic energy up from your feet and into your root chakra, and then suspend the breath for a moment, feeling the energy collect at the base of your spine as you focus your awareness of your inner tone to the sensation you feel around your tailbone.

Step 3. Exhale gently while keeping your attention and your inner tone set at the location of your root chakra and let the energy expand and begin to open up.

Step 4. Repeat steps 2. and 3. until you feel the energy in your root chakra open up completely. This will feel like you're sitting on a cloud and the cloud is raining out all of the tension in your pelvic area.

We use the root chakra for grounding, it is also the foundation of the chakra tower in our energy body and the anchoring point of our energy as we open up to the higher chakras in the body. We must ground our energy, through the root chakra, to prevent energy from getting "stuck" in our body as we move through and open up the energy body. Visualize roots growing down into the Earth or water pouring out of a pitcher as you let the old energy fall away. When your energy is grounded and your root shock rough is comfortably open it becomes like a guide for energy to the other shock risk.

We also draw healing energy up from mother earth in our practices and the root chakra is the gatekeeper.

EXERCISE 4. RISING SUN

Step 1. Begin by setting your inner tone to the frequency of your root chakra and guiding energy into the chakra with your pranic breath until your root chakra is fully and comfortably open.

Step 2. On the inhale of your breath cycle raise your inner tone from your root chakra up to where your sacral chakra is located, just below the belly button in the pelvic area. Breathe into the chakra when you begin to feel it tingling and then move the tone back down to the root chakra and repeat until you pull in enough energy from the root to open up the sacral chakra.

Step 3. With the root and sacral chakras both open, and on the inhale of your breath cycle, guide your inner tone up from your root and through your sacral chakra to the area in your solar plexus. Suspend your inner tone for a moment at the point where you feel your solar plexus chakra energizing and then exhale, feeling the energy begin to open up, and then dropping your breath back down to the root chakra on your exhale as you hold the tone in your solar plexus chakra. Repeat this process, pulling pranic energy up from your root and through your sacral chakra with abdominal breathing, until the solar plexus chakra is fully cleared and open. At any point you can lower the tone from your solar plexus to attach to the rising energy and pull it up to the solar plexus chakra by raising the tone again to the frequency of that chakra.

Step 4. With the lower three chakras open, begin raising the tone from your solar plexus chakra to your heart chakra located in the middle of your chest. Hold your inner tone at the location of the heart chakra, bring your awareness to the energy in the lower chakras as you exhale, and inhale abdominally as you fill up and draw the prana into your heart chakra. As the heart opens, relax the breath as you exhale, and feel your energy body opening and expanding throughout these four chakras.

Step 5. With the four lower chakras open, move your inner tone and your awareness up-and-down throughout your energy body to gain awareness of the sensations and to practice tonal control. End the exercise by shifting your attention from your inner tone to the simple awareness of sensation you're feeling and relax your breathing by settling into the feeling of the energy in your root chakra.

This exercise builds a strong foundation for opening the higher chakras and will help us in grounding and balancing the stronger energies of these chakras. We can use our inner tone to pull energy to the root chakra and ground it to the earth. As we fill up our body from the root chakra up to the heart chakra with prana and let the heart chakra open fully, an expansion of energy occurs that goes beyond the body and we want to keep this energy grounded by paying attention to both the root and the heart chakra at the same time. Practice this exercise until you can easily open the lower part of your energy body and expand your heart chakra fully.

EXERCISE 5. RAISING THE TOWER

Step 1. Begin with the rising sun exercise and open the first four chakras, and your energy body, up to the heart chakra.

Step 2. Bring your inner tone into your heart chakra and then raise it to the frequency of your throat chakra as you draw pranic breath from your root chakra, up through the heart chakra to the throat chakra located at the middle of your neck in the throat area.

Step 3. Suspend your inner tone in your throat chakra, exhale and let the energy expand, up from the heart, into the throat chakra, and back down to the root chakra, filling your energy body up with prana from the root chakra to the throat chakra with every breath until the throat chakra opens.

Step 4. Raise the frequency of your inner tone from your throat chakra to your third eye chakra, located in the center and toward the front of your head, as you pull your pranic breath from the root chakra, up through the throat chakra, and into your inner tone in the middle of your head. Exhale and let the energy expand in your third eye chakra, and fall back into your root chakra, as you hold your inner tone to the frequency of your third eye chakra, feeling the chakra begin to expand on your exhale. Continue "pulling" prana into the third eye chakra, with abdominal breathing, until the third eye chakra fully opens up with the other chakras, and continue.

Step 5. Repeat the pattern, raising your inner tone up to the area at the top of your head to where you feel your crown chakra start tingling, hold the tone, and let the energy expand and release into the crown chakra and then back down through the chakras. Feel your open heart as energy falls back to your root chakra on the exhale and repeat the pattern until your crown chakra opens fully.

Step 6. With your whole energy body now open, slowly lower your inner tone, and your awareness, back down to the root chakra and up again, bringing your awareness to each chakra as you continue to scan up and down your chakra column.

Step 7. Slowly let your inner tone diminish and bring your focus back outside of your body, you can move your fingers or tap your feet, while you do your best to remain aware of the openness you feel in your body.

This exercise helps identify and open the upper chakras in the body. As we open our crown chakra and then bring our awareness back to the root chakra our energy body will open completely with all the chakras in the body flowing energy freely thru our chakra tower allowing us to move energy throughout our energy body. With your energy body fully open, bring your attention to any place in need of healing and allow the energy there to "unlock" and flow through, grounding the energy by breathing into it and releasing.

Practice your manifestation techniques with your energy body fully open and you will see faster results, especially when projecting your desires through the solar plexus chakra. Allow this energy to permeate and expand as far as is comfortable, pushing the limits a little bit each time you practice and then grounding the excess energy back to mother Earth.

Take your time and experiment with your tonal movement and have fun. Spend some time to gain proficiency in these exercises before moving on to the more advanced techniques, always remembering to clear old energy before bringing new energy in and to stay grounded as you navigate the higher chakras. As you move energy in the same patterns through your energy body, you begin to widen the pranic pathways allowing you to open each chakra easier every time you practice.

"You can have peace of mind, improved health, and an ever increasing flow of energy. Life can be full of joy and satisfaction." - Norman Vincent Peale

INNER TONAL NAVIGATION

Now we begin to get creative with our inner tone. So far we have learned to move our inner tone up and down the vertical axis of our body along the spinal column. Now we will learn how to move our inner tone out from our core horizontally, to 360° around the body, by adjusting the volume between the left and right ear and by shifting our awareness of tonal location within our energy body. With practice you can isolate any part of your energy body with awareness of your tonal location and move energy to that location for clearing, healing, and revitalizing any of your muscles, joints, and organs, and your entire body. With our body completely energized our auric field can be fully realized.

Our auras extend beyond our physical body. Interacting with our energy field outside our body benefits us in many ways. We communicate with the subtle energies of the quantum field at this level of connection, increasing our awareness on all levels. When we identify with this expanded awareness of ourselves, our understanding and awareness of a unified field of consciousness is expanded as well. Just as a telescope reveals a multitude of universes where the naked eye sees only darkness, the expanded identity begins to reveal the limitless essence of your being to the furthest of your imagination. Use the exercises that follow to move beyond your body and to map every inch of your aura as well. Mastery will bring instant activation of your whole energy field in one breath. This is where we truly shine. Life is experienced as an extension of your being with the awareness of your connection to the whole of everything.

Imagine what it would be like to be a giant bell. When you strike your tone the sound rings out in every direction. In that moment the bell and the sound exists in the same vibration at the same time. As far as the sound of the bell can be heard it is still connected to its source. Of course the sound of the bell is restricted by the laws of the physical universe and can only travel so far. The quantum field however is connected to all points of space and time in the now a moment. In that moment you are the source and the destination. The breadth and scope of your reach is only as far as your imagination. Then, at the moment when you think you can't reach any further, you surrender to find you are already there.

Consider doing tonal work like working out. Isolation and repetition of training for different muscles over time brings strength and conditioning. So it is for opening your energy body. Just like strength training it is important to work all your muscle groups. This means mapping your entire energetic field with your inner tone, bringing you full body and energy awareness.

EXERCISE 6. FIRE ENGINE

Step 1. Set your inner tone at the center of your awareness.

Step 2. Imagine a fire engine siren and match your inner tone to the sound of the siren in your inner ear.

Step 3. Become aware of the location of your inner tone rising and lowering within your energy body.

This exercise brings our awareness to the energy body as we begin to feel our inner tone moving up-and-down our spine. This awareness is the starting point for every other exercise in this book.

EXERCISE 7. PANNING

Step 1. Set your inner tone at the center of your awareness.

Step 2. Raise the volume of the tone in your right ear as you place your attention to the tone as if it were coming from the location of the right ear.

Step 3. Shift your attention back to the middle of your head as you lower the volume of the right ear, setting your inner tone back to center.

Step 4. Raise the volume of the tone in your left ear and place your attention there, just as you did at the right ear, "hearing" the tone in the left ear.

Step 5. Shift your attention back to the center of your awareness and equalize the volume of the tone in each ear and then repeat the process.

This technique is called "panning" in recording studios, when you create movement of sound from the left to right speaker, or vice-versa, by lowering the volume of one speaker and then raising the volume on the opposite speaker. This exercise helps us begin to move our inner tone horizontally through the energy body. We use pitch to move our inner tone vertically and we use our awareness to move our inner tone horizontally. Using pitch and awareness together can place the inner tone anywhere in our energy body.

EXERCISE 8. FRONT TO BACK

Step 1. Set your inner tone at the center of your awareness.

Step 2. Begin to draw the tone forward with your awareness, hearing it in your inner ear as if It is being held out in front of you.

Step 3. Move the tone back to center, paying attention to the location of the tone as it travels through your energy body.

Step 4. Draw the tone toward the back of your head by "hearing" the tone, in your mind, coming from a location behind your head.

Step 5. Bring the tone back to the center of your awareness, paying attention as it returns to the center of your head, then repeat.

This exercise helps to bring further control of the movement of our inner tone away from the central axis of our energy body and brings awareness to the energy outside of our physical body. The same principle of panning applies to this exercise as well, once you have established the tone at the front or the back from the center, you can then adjust the volume of tone between the front and back of your head to move the tone in either direction.

An example would be setting your inner tone to your solar plexus, then using your awareness to "pull" the tone toward your belly button, by imagining the source of the tone coming from outside your body and in front of your stomach.

This exercise requires a stretch of the imagination. You are literally beginning to bring awareness to your "self outside of yourself". Everything is energy and the perceived boundaries we attach to our bodies can be dissolved. When you begin to identify yourself with the empty space around you, the connection to the quantum field becomes undeniable. There is no limit to your expansion.

EXERCISE 9. FULL CIRCLE

Step 1. Draw the tone of your inner ear from the center of your awareness to the back of your head and then adjust the volume of the tone in your right ear as you move the tone, with your awareness, in a semicircle from the back of your head to your right ear. Reverse and repeat until it feels like you are beginning to draw a circle of sound around your head.

Step 2. Repeat this process on the left hemisphere, drawing the tone from the back of your head to the left ear and back again. Once you have established this tonal path, continue from the left ear, through the center of your awareness at the back of your head to the right ear and back again, creating a half circle from ear to ear around the back of your head.

Step 3. Draw your inner tone from center to the area in front of your face and turn up the volume of your right ear as you guide the tone, with your awareness, in a semicircle around the front of your face to your right ear and back again.

Step 4. With your attention front and center, draw your inner tone from the front of your face to the left ear by adjusting the volume of your left ear to draw the tone in a semicircle around your face from the front to left and back again. Once you become aware of the tonal movement from the front of your face to your left ear then back again continue around the front of your face to complete a half circle from the left ear to the right ear and back again.

Step 5. Draw your inner tone from the center of your awareness to the back of the head and starting with step 1. begin to move the tone In a full circle around your head. Picture yourself drawing a circle with a pencil and imagine the tip of that pencil is where your awareness intersects with your inner tone.

This exercise helps us to harmonize the left and right hemispheres of our brain as well as our energy body. It is important that we balance both hemispheres as we work on opening up our energy body. The chakras are fused with the nervous system, the nervous system communicates with the brain, and balance keeps the lines of communication open to every cell in the body and to every facet of our spirit.

EXERCISE 10. FIGURE EIGHT

Step 1. Set your inner tone at the center of your awareness.

Step 2. Move the tone up to the top of your head, then down toward your right ear, and back to the top in a loop.

Step 3. Continue the movement of your inner tone over the top of your head and down toward your left ear, and then loop the tone back to the top of your head and over to loop down toward your right ear and back again creating a figure eight of tonal movement across the inside of the top of your head.

Step 4. Guide the figure eight tonal movement slowly to the front, and then to the back of your head, massaging your brain as you go.

This exercise balances the right and left hemispheres of the brain while stimulating its circuitry from the inside out, repairing damaged cells and optimizing performance.

EXERCISE 11. CHOIR OF ANGELS

Step 1. Set your inner tone to the center of your awareness.

Step 2. Begin to "ping pong" your inner tone to different locations up and down your spine by changing the pitch of your inner tone, along with your awareness of the location of the tone in your body, to the frequencies of the different chakras. An example would be to move your inner tone from your heart to your root, root to crown, crown to sacral, sacral to throat, throat to solar plexus, and so on.

Step 3. Keep your awareness of the frequency of your inner tone at one location as you add the next tone to that frequency so that you are aware of, or are "hearing", both tones at the same time and continue the process of "adding" tones until you can sustain the tones of all of the chakras frequencies at the same time.

This exercise trains your awareness to multiple tones at the same time. This is an exercise in multi dimensionality, this exercise can activate all of your chakras in one breath and open your energy body in an instant.

FULL TONAL CONTROL

As you adjust the volume, pitch, and location of tone through awareness, you move your inner tone through your energy body. Your inner tone can lead you to awareness of any part of your physical body and anywhere in the field of your energy body and with practice you can move your awareness of your inner tone to your left ear lobe, your right knee, or your little pinky.

When you bring pranic breath to the awareness of your organs, muscles and joints you start to release toxins and bring healing and rejuvenating energy to anyplace in the body you choose. When we use our inner tone to guide energy through our bodies we are gradually "mapping" the body as we bring fresh energy to stagnant areas in our energy field that may not have seen the light of day in some time.

When practicing tonal movement throughout your energy body you will experience sensations of pleasure, tingling, tickling and joy. Yes joy, joy has quite an ecstatic feeling on a quantum level and sometimes it may feel as if it wants to take your breath away.. In time these sensations will become more manageable as your body gets used to the new energy.

"If you carry joy in your heart, you can heal any moment."
-Carlos Santana

CHAKRAS OUTSIDE OF THE BODY

Our physical bodies only resonate within a small frequency spectrum of reality. This spectral range is what we call the third and fourth dimension where objects can be measured and compared across space and time.

Beyond that we have the astral body, also called the emotional, etheric, or light body among other names. Experiencing the activation of the astral body moves us into the 4th dimension (the "now" moment in time). The 4th dimension is the realization of the connection of ourselves to non-physical reality and the awareness of our own spiritual essence.

When your crown chakra is open you are experiencing 4th dimensional frequencies and a sense of yourself outside of yourself. We also experienced the 4th dimension in out of body experiences and dreams, where we have a sense of ourselves outside of our body yet we are also aware of time, space and 3rd dimensional emotional vibrations such as confusion or fear.

As we raise our vibration to the 5th dimension we lose awareness of any lower vibrations of the third and fourth dimensions as we tap into source energy, the energy that sustains and affects the quantum field, where we experience "heaven on earth", bliss, nirvana and complete absolution into spirit.

We can raise our frequency to the 5th dimension by opening the soul star chakra, located about twelve inches above the top of your head. The frequency of the soul star chakra is (1074 Hz) and its color is white, the color of the other seven chakras combined. Called the seat of the soul, the 8th chakra takes us from the connection of the individual to spirit, that we find in the crown chakra, to the experience of "being" spirit.

As the soul star is above, the Earth star is below. The Earth star chakra is located 8-12 inches below the feet and connects us to the center of the planet; this is where we ground our energy through our root chakra. The frequency of the soul star chakra is (68.05 Hz), which is barely audible, and it is dark brown or black in color. The Earth star chakra is the anchor for all the other chakras, in our body and beyond, and it connects us to all humanity.

In the exercises that follow begin with your energy body fully open and end by grounding your energy back to the Earth star. As your energy moves in any direction with your breath it may want to pull back, especially when you are charting new territory in your energy body. You can save the progression of your energy along its path by holding your inner tone while pulling your belly in and tightening your abdominal muscles
slightly as you exhale, then inhale as you continue to move the energy along to the next chakra.

EXERCISE 12. EARTHBOUND

Step 1. Start in a sitting position with your energy body open and bring your awareness to your root chakra.

Step 2. Lower your inner tone down from your root chakra toward the bottom of your feet until the tone becomes inaudible. At this point bring your awareness even further down past the bottom of your feet by sensing the subtle magnetic pull of the Earth below until you feel as if you're standing on the bottom of an energy bubble that surrounds your whole body.

Step 3. Breathe into the belly and then exhale, Letting the magnetism of the planet connect to, and pull your energy down to your Earth star chakra, grounding your energy body. Now bring your tonal awareness back to your heart chakra as you inhale, filling the heart with prana and then exhale, shifting your tonal awareness back down to your root chakra and guiding your energy back down to the planet at your Earth star chakra and repeating the pattern until you feel a balanced flow of energy between your heart chakra and your Earth star chakra.

Step 4. Settle and balance your energy throughout your energy body while bringing your tonal awareness back to your heart chakra. Breathe with your belly and relax into the sensations you are feeling.

This exercise helps us build a strong foundation for grounding our energy. The Earth star chakra balances the energy in our bodies and allows us to bring cosmic energy down through our star chakra and into our bodies. We feel stable and more a part of humanity with a strong connection to our Earth star chakra.

There are endless levels of energy awareness traveling up-and-down from our primary chakra tower. When higher frequencies come into our Crown chakra they must be able to flow through our Earth star to keep the stronger energy moving. As your energy body accumulates to higher frequencies, more energy wants to come in. If you can keep your Earth star chakra open you become an open conduit for cosmic energy.

EXERCISE 13. THE LIGHT ABOVE

Step 1. With your energy body fully open bring your tonal awareness to the frequency of your crown chakra.

Step 2. Raise your inner tone, feeling the sensation rise up from the top of your head as you fill your belly with air on your inhale and then exhale allowing pranic energy to follow your inner tonal path up to your star chakra located 8-12 inches above your head. Repeat this process until you feel your star chakra open up, then bring your tonal awareness down to your solar plexus chakra on your inhale, and continue down to your Earth star chakra on your exhale.

Step 3. With the soul star chakra and the Earth star chakra now activated continue the exercise by bringing your awareness from your soul star chakra to your solar plexus on your inhale, and then exhaling, bringing your awareness, with your inner tone, down from your solar plexus to your Earth star chakra, cycling your energy with your breath through the seven chakras in your body as you breathe slowly in through the nose and out through the mouth.

This exercise connects us to the cosmos bringing us spiritual and multi-dimensional experiences, opening our minds to our connection to the quantum field and our oneness with everyone and everything. We move from one who is experiencing spirit to "one with" spirit, an awareness so expensive that the feeling of the body becomes a feeling of embodiment.

There are no barriers to your expansion. With an expanded presence comes greater awareness. With greater awareness comes a deeper understanding of life and your place in it, or the other way around. Understanding allows more flexibility and less fear of the unknown. This cycle releasing and expanding into more awareness eventually leads to a place where all secrets are revealed and there is nothing to fear.

EXERCISE 14. WHALE SONG

Step1. Open up your energy body and settle into a comfortable and rhythmic breathing pattern.

Step 2. Bring your awareness to your crown chakra with a slow inhalation into your belly. Suspend your breath momentarily then exhale with the movement of your energy. Let the full range of the song travel through your energy body.

Step 4. Let the whale song play on its own as you become the listener. Relax and breathe with the movement of energy through your body as the pitch falls from beautiful arias to other wordly subsonic undertones.

This exercise gives us a glimpse into the ability of our innate capacity to guide energy and heal our bodies. As we let go and listen we become the observer we see that energy goes right where it needs to effortlessly. Each whale song is unique, it is like a fingerprint, strengthening our authenticity and connecting us to mother Earth.

EXERCISE 15. PYRAMID OF LIGHT

Step 1. With your energy body fully open and grounded bring your tonal awareness to your crown chakra.

Step 2. Envision a pyramid forming down and around your body from your crown chakra to the ground.

Step 3. Trace the formation lines of the pyramid from your body to the ground one at a time. Begin on either side of your body and lower your inner tone down and away from your body. Let the formation line and your tone reach further down with each exhale until you connect with the earth at a location a few feet out from your center.

Step 4. Remain aware of this first line of energy as one corner of a pyramid and repeat the process on the other side of your body. Once you have the sides connected from crown to ground continue to the front and back of the pyramid until all 4 edges of the pyramid are completely connected.

Step 5. Hold the pyramid formation and begin to fill the space within with pranic energy. Let the energy come in from your crown and heart chakras simultaneously as the inside of your pyramid fills from the bottom up.

This exercise help to fortify your tonal bilocation abilities while building a strong foundation energetically. You may see a pyramid outline in your mind's eyes as you complete the process.

We are limitless and when we begin to go beyond ourselves

to higher realms of consciousness the sacred geometry of the pyramid helps keep our energy in alignment.

" The pyramid shape is said to hold many secrets and amazing properties. One of them is a sense of wonder". - Vera Nazaran

EXPLORING THE ENERGY BODY

Now that we have full awareness of our energy body let's have some fun with our inner tone. You can use the exercises for inner tonal control as a starting point but remember you are the director of your own inner tone.

You can move your inner tone down your arms and legs if you wish, Imagine you're wearing a "suit" of energy. You can build tonal "chords", sustaining two or more chakra tones at the same time, to open up communication between the two chakras. If you inhale prana into your third eye chakra and exhale that energy through your heart and out of the front of your solar plexus chakra you literally charge ambient energy with love and return it back to the quantum field. If you can imagine hearing all of the chakra frequencies at once, like sustaining all the notes of a keyboard at the same time (choir of angels), you will feel your whole body light up at once. Start slowly and be creative, It's your body and it's your consciousness that sustains it. Now you have the tools to bring harmony and balance to your mental, emotional and physical reality through a balanced and open chakra system.

CLEARING ENERGY

Clearing energy is just as important as moving energy when working to open our chakras and our energy body. If you can imagine water trying to flow through a clogged pipe you will have an idea of the flow of energy in your body when there are blockages present. Just as pressure builds up in a pipe when it is clogged we feel pressure and discomfort in our body at the point of any blockages in our "pipes".

We have already learned to ground our energy through the root chakra and with our crown chakra open we can let energy rise up from the top of our head. Excess energy in your body is either going to want to flow up or down.

Let your energy flow in the direction it wants to naturally while remembering to stay grounded. More often than not you will want to lower your inner tone from the blockage as you exhale and relax, letting the stuck energy fall back down through your root chakra and into the Earth star.

You can pull energy up through your feet and to the blockage to "grab" a bit of the stuck energy and let it fall back down to the Earth star on your exhale. Repeat this until the blockage is cleared and you can feel the energy flow freely.

SELF HEALING

Any pain, discomfort, or disease in your body is a result of a distortion in your natural flow of life force energy. The causes of these distortions are numerous. They affect different systems of the body but they all leave trauma well after the initial injury or symptom has healed.

As your energy body opens, distortions in your field become easier to identify. You will feel them like little islands of space where your energy just flows around it and doesn't want to penetrate. When you become aware of any blockages in your field you can release them with your clearing exercise. Imagine that the energy moving down your spine is like a river and your body is a canyon. You will find that every point of awareness in your energy body can be connected to your spine just as a tributary flows to a river.

To clear any blockages start with your energy body open. Move your inner tone from your spine to the blockage and breathe into it. Let the energy expand and dissipate, like an ice cube melting into water and then turning into steam. Let the expanded energy flow back into the spine and down to the ground on your exhale. Keep breathing, creating a pathway that literally sucks the energy from the blockage as it is released. Continue to pull the expanded energy from the blockage to the spine, siphoning and grounding until you feel relief. This brings comfort to the general area of your body that you are working with. It also allows more energy to flow to other areas of the body that may have been neglected.

There is a blueprint for your natural state of being and when your frequency is in tune with it, your body will conform to it. This return to perfection may not happen overnight though you will feel relief immediately. Some injuries, generally older ones, have been deprived of vital life force for so long that they may take more work than others to restore harmony.

Chronic joint pain can be especially fun to work with. These areas can feel dead to the rest of the body except for when the pain comes. When you go in there with your inner tone, open it up and let the light shine in, the pain turns to pleasure. This fresh energy brings ecstatic sensations of rebirth to whatever area of your body being healed. Opening up energy in your joints will adjust your skeleton back to its original form. Bringing your inner tone into any stretching routine is a wonderful way to isolate blockages. You can really pinpoint your body awareness which makes any tension an easy target for you to set your inner tone and begin releasing tension.

Each of your organs have a specific frequency as well. When you move your inner tone through your body, you are moving through the frequencies of your organs by default. When you apply the same healing principle as before you get the same result. Bringing the breath of life into any organ and unlocking and releasing stuck energy will make space for fresh, healing, life force energy to fill the void. Remember that each one of your organs is governed by a correlating chakra. Absorb stagnant energy from the organ into the chakra and then clear that chakra with the stream of energy running through your body and grounding.

As you begin to clean all the junk out of your body it begins to morph back into the pristine blueprint of its creation. Your body returns to its innate form and remembrance of its true power and ability. Everyone's body is different with a different past and a different medical record. Your body will want to do things its own way. Just let your inner tone guide the breath to the area of your body that is in need of activation and healing and let your innate give you clues on how to proceed. When you master your frequency you control every molecule in your body and nothing is impossible.

Emotional trauma is stored in the layer of our energy body called the emotional body. Different emotions are expressed through different chakras. Emotions such as happiness or sadness are not opposites, they are merely different amplitudes of the frequency of joy. Joy is a quality of love and love is the base frequency of creation. Love is like light and creation is like light hitting the atmosphere and making rainbows. To help with emotional trauma it's best to bring yourself to a place of deep relaxation. Open up The chakra you want to work with and just sit with whatever comes up. Become the observer and let the wisdom of your innate being take over. Bathe in the light.

EGREGORES

In your healing process it is important to remember that we are not the source of our habitual emotional and/or mental disturbances. Feelings or thoughts of depression, anxiety, guilt, and unworthiness are merely potential frequencies of a collective mind. If you're depressed you're not the only one. You are however tuning into the same frequency as every other human on the planet that is depressed. If you are experiencing great joy you can be sure that you're sharing that moment with everyone else tuned into that same frequency of joy in that moment and across time.

Have you ever gone out not feeling like you were going to have a good time? You get to a party and start mingling with the other people that are having fun. Before you know it you're feeling great and you're glad that you came out after all. The collective vibration of fun and celebration raised your frequency because it was the most prevalent atmosphere of your experience.

That's how the tonal chakra development system works. It's the higher frequencies of the heart chakra that opens up and heals our body. It's our ability to guide that healing light, through our energy body with our inner tone, that liberates us from the frequency of trauma/karma accumulated through attachments to dysfunctional egregores. Just like the party, when you raise the vibration of the "room" (your energy body), the disgruntled "party goer" (your pain and trauma) experiences health and well-being.

Be mindful of your thoughts as your chakras begin to open. The energy that you're clearing is trauma stuck in your body. It is helpful to let any emotions that come up be expressed. Let your body and your heart feel everything from a detached perspective. Become an observer. Laugh on the inside as you cry on the outside. Remember, these traumas are not a product of you, they are frequencies available and common to all. They are in your field of awareness because they weren't processed properly. The music of your divinity is trapped behind a wall of noise and all you have to do to move on is change your tune.

TRAINING AIDS

While the tonal chakra development system is designed to train you in generating and modulating your own inner tone there are tools to help you identify your inner tone and the different frequencies therein. It could be as simple as the microwave beeping or as obvious as striking a key on a piano. When you are using an outside tone to initiate your inner tone there are a few steps to take.

1) Harmonize your inner ear to the tone you are listening to.

2) Bring your awareness to the area of the body where you feel the tone.

3) Turn off the outside source of the tone as you sustain your inner tone.

The main benefit of harmonizing your inner tone with an outside source, such as a keyboard, is to set the tone at the precise frequency of each chakra and become familiar with these tones so that with practice we can instantly generate these same frequencies with our inner ear.

VOICE

Although our vocal range may be limited, most of us can hit the notes required to activate our energy centers from our solar plexus to our throat chakra. Chanting has been used for thousands of years to help induce a meditative or "trance" state of being through sound and vibration (frequency). Om is chanted before and after meditations by Hindu yogis and Buddhist monks. The three syllables *a-u-m* which represent the three worlds of earth, atmosphere and heaven; the three qualities of thought, speech and action; and other significant triads.

The vowels *a* and *u* come together to sound an *o* and closes out with an *m* sound. It is a sacred syllable and is considered to be the greatest of all mantras. We can use these tools and more to help us associate a tone to a location in our body through vibration.

When you hum a tune and you raise or lower the tone you will feel a vibration in your body moving also. Singing is very helpful in opening the throat chakra. Sing consciously and notice the subtle sensations in your energy body. Sing again in your mind with an awareness of those same sensations until your inner tone harmonizes with the frequency of the vibration in your energy body.

MUSICAL INSTRUMENTS

The instruments of modern orchestral music, including the piano and the guitar, are generally tuned to 440 Hz at or above the A note.

An alternative tuning exists which gives the A note a frequency of 432 Hz. This tuning is believed to be in a more harmonic relationship with nature and mathematically entwined with the sacred geometry of the universe. 432 Hz is also the frequency of the root chakra, which makes it a better candidate for relating musical notes to the frequencies of our chakras.

The frequencies of the corresponding musical notes beyond the root chakra will come close to the frequencies of your other chakras but will not be a perfect match. The notes of the musical scales are meant to be representations of their correlating chakras and can be used to get you close enough to your chakras frequency to let your intuition take over and find perfect harmony.

NOTES IN THE KEY OF CHAKRA

Chakra	Note
Root: (432 Hz)	A4 (432 Hz)
Sacral: (480 Hz)	B4 (484.9 Hz)
Solar plexus: (528 Hz)	C5 (513.74Hz)
Heart: (594 Hz)	D5 (587.33Hz)
Throat: (672 Hz)	E5 (659.25Hz)
Third eye: (720 Hz)	F5 (698.46Hz)
Crown: (768 Hz)	G5 (769.74Hz)

Note: The frequencies of the given are in 432 standard tuning.

THE SOLFEGGIO SCALE

The solfeggio scale is a six tone scale dating back to the 11th century that is believed to be in tune with the frequencies of nature and have mystical and healing properties.

It is the scale used in Gregorian chants of old and the tones of the solfeggio scale are used today in meditation music and sound healing.

The frequencies of the solfeggio scale are given in the description of each chakra and you can find the tones with Tibetan singing bowls or a frequency generator.

FREQUENCY GENERATOR

A frequency generator manufactures a tone that you can adjust manually to the different frequencies of the chakras. You can download a frequency generator app on your cell phone and turn your presets to the frequencies of the different chakras in your body. Once you harmonize your inner ear with the frequency generator, practice by turning the frequency generator off while sustaining the frequency with your inner ear at the location of the chakra, or chakras, that you are paying attention to.

This tool is to be used only as a training modality. Once you are aware of your tonal location interfacing with your chakras, let your innate fine tune your energy with the tone that you are generating.

TIBETAN SINGING BOWLS

Tibetan singing bowls have been used by the Buddhist monks for centuries to enhance their meditations. The bowls produce tones that activate the chakras and can be used as a tool to familiarize yourself with these tones and learn to generate the same tones with your inner ear.

Meditation and immersion into the sacred tones offered by these musical bowls is a doorway to Enlightenment. Harmonize your energy body to the frequencies of the bowls with your inner ear and become the tones. This is a very blissful, relaxing, and easy way to familiarize yourself with the healing frequencies you are exploring.

IMAGINATION

Use your imagination, find songs you like in different keys that relate to the different chakras, try feeling what chakras are activated by the different sounds you hear in a day. It is your imagination, your awareness, that is necessary to master control of your inner tone after all so be creative and have fun.

Our thoughts, having frequencies of their own, create our reality. When you use the power of imagination with intended vibration, you are playing your role as a co-creator Of reality. You manifest life with awareness, choosing the frequencies you wish to participate in.

"Reality leaves a lot to the imagination." - John Lennon

PRACTICE HELPS THE WORLD GO 'ROUND

As was said before, we relate to the quantum field through our energy bodies, we share this energy with everything and everyone in existence. When our energy body is open we are bringing more "light" energy into the quantum field, enlightening reality for the whole. Consider this while you're walking, standing in line, or at a stop light. Anytime you think of it you can open your heart chakra and bless everything around you. You will become more in tune with the subtle energies around you as you begin to open up your own energy body, and when you bring light into any equation It helps everyone involved in any situation.

You will find more and more people smiling at you as you walk down the street because their energy can sense the light in your energy and they feel better just by looking at you. You will begin to enjoy this, opening up your chakras all the time, and soon enough you will be able to activate your energy body with just the thought of it and start living the blessings and miracles that are your birthright.

"Drop by drop is the water pot filled." - Buddha

About the author

Dan Schoeffler lives in Nevada City, California and is now enjoying a life of vibrant health and loving relationships with his friends and family. Dan's quest of self-healing and awakening began in the winter of 2018 after he was hospitalized due to liver failure and diagnosed with alcoholic cirrhosis, alcoholic hepatitis, and stage 5 kidney damage. After a few days in the hospital Dan was released and told that he was being put on a list for a liver transplant and to see a doctor again in a month for an evaluation. With nothing to do but lay in bed Dan decided to start meditating again, he discovered sound-healing audio tracks online and dedicated a few hours a day to practicing these self-healing modalities for his recovery. A month passed and Dan was at the doctor's office for his evaluation. After reviewing the data from the (CT) scan the doctor asked Dan what he had done to improve his health so profoundly in such a short period of time. Dan's liver was now too healthy to perform a transplant. So began a journey of healing and self-discovery that brought about the epiphanies and revelations put forth in this manual.

Glossary

akash-ic re-cord: In the religion of theosophy and the philosophical school called anthroposophy, the acoustic records are a compendium of all universal events, thoughts, words, emotions and intent ever to have occurred in the past, present, or future in terms of all entities and life forms, not just human.

as-tral trav-el: an esoteric term used to describe an out of body experience (OBE) that assumes the existence of a subtle body called an "astral body" through which consciousness can function separately from the physical body and travel throughout the astral plane.

a-ware-ness: knowledge of a situation or fact.

bi-o-e-lec-tri-ci-ty: the flow of electrical currents, carried by mobile charge ions, across cell membranes and along the exterior and interior ionic environment of cells.

bliss: perfect happiness, great joy.

cha-kra: (in Indian thought) each of the centers of spiritual power in the human body, usually considered to be seven in number.

e-lec-tro-mag-net-ic field: a field of force that consists of both electric and magnetic components, resulting from the motion of an electric charge and containing a definite amount of electromagnetic energy.

fre-quen-cy: 1. The rate at which something occurs or is repeated over a particular period of time or in a given sample. 2. the rate at which a vibration occurs that constitutes a wave, either in a material (as in sound waves), or in an electromagnetic field (as in radio waves and light), usually measured per second.

hertz: A unit of frequency equal to one cycle per second.

prana: breath, considered as a life giving force.

res-on-ance: 1. The quality in a sound of being deep, full, and reverberating. 2. The reinforcement or prolongation of sound by reflection from a surface or by the synchronist vibration of a neighboring object.

quan-tum: a discreet quality of energy proportional in magnitude to the frequency of the radiation it represents.

whale-song: terminology for the variety of sounds used by whales for communication and sensation.

A BEGINNER'S GUIDE TO TONAL CHAKRA DEVELOPMENT

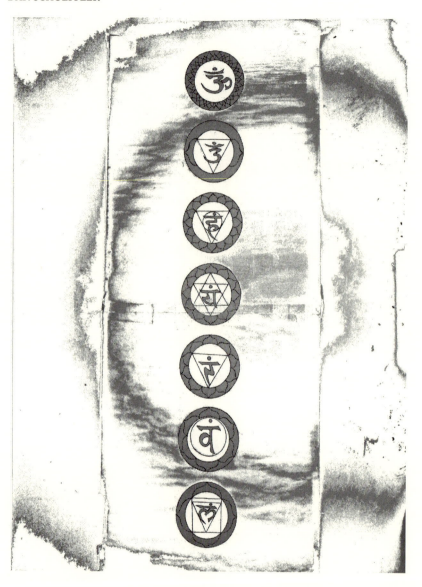

As I dissolve into spirit I find

There is nowhere I am not

And here is only

Where I Am

DAN SCHOEFFLER

A BEGINNER'S GUIDE TO TONAL CHAKRA DEVELOPMENT

Made in the USA
Middletown, DE
26 September 2022